Divinizing of Human Being
(Means and Method According to Yogavāsiṣṭha)

I0217407

By
Dr. Ravi Prakash Arya

AMAZON BOOKS, USA

in association with

INDIAN FOUNDATION FOR VEDIC SCIENCE
1051, Sector-1, Rohtak, Haryana, India Ph. 01262-292580
Delhi Contact Ph. Nos.: 09313033917; 9650183260
Emails: vedicscience@rediffmail.com
vedicscience@hotmail.com
Website : www.vedicscience.net

First Edition

Christian era: 2015
Vikram era: 2072
Kali era: 5116
Kalpa Era: 1972949116
Brahma Era: 155521972949116

ISBN No. 81-87710-91-8

INTRODUCTION

Yogavāsiṣṭha is a very bulky size famous book on Indian philosophy. It is known by several names, e.g. Mahārāmāyaṇa, Ārṣarāmāyaṇa, Vasiṣṭharāmāyaṇa, Jñānavāsiṣṭha or Vāsiṣṭha. This work has six chapters known as Prakaraṇas. They may be enumerated as under :

Vairāgya Prakaraṇa-This describes disillusionment with world. The issue discussed here is whether jñāna (enlightenment) or karma (willful action) is more important in attaining liberation. The answer is that both are equally important, just as a bird needs both wings to fly.

1. *Mumukṣu Vyvahāra Prakaraṇa-* This describes the qualities of a true seeker and his mental attitude.

2. *Utpatti Prakaraṇa-* This describes as to how the world was created and how it evolved.

3. *Sthiti Prakaraṇa-* This describes how the world is sustained.

4. *Upaśama Prakaraṇa-*This describes how the mind is quietened through proper understanding.

5. *Nirvāṇa Prakaraṇa-* This is about liberation. It suggests that realization of Brahm is the best way to liberation.

Nirvāṇa prakaraṇa is further divided into two parts Purvārdha (first half) and Uttarārdha (second half). It is as large as first five combined.

As per description of *Yogavāsiṣṭha*, this work contains 32,000 ślokas.

mokṣopāyābhidhāneyaṁ saṁhitā sārasṁmitā
triṁśat dve ca sahasrāṇī Jñātā nirvāṇa-dāyini. (2.17.6)

But the manuscript of *Yogavāsiṣṭha* preserved in the India Office library of London contains 28660 *ślokas.* The *Yogavāsiṣṭ ha* published from Nirṇaya Sāgar press Bombay contains 27687 *ślokas.* Though several other manuscripts are available, but all of them are incomplete and fragmentary. Form time to time, scholars have been producing the *Yogavāsiṣṭha* in fragments as per their interests and objectives. Today *Yogavāsiṣṭha* is available in the market in the following pocket size editions, e.g.

Laghu Yogavāsiṣṭha

Yogavāsiṣṭha śloka

Yogavāsiṣṭha sāra

Vāsiṣṭha sāra

Jñanavāsiṣṭha samuccaya etc.

We come across several commentaries on *Yogavāsiṣṭha.* Advayāraṇya son of Narahari attempted his commentary on the *Yogavāsiṣṭha* in the name of *Vāsiṣtha Rāmāyaṇā.* In nineteenth century, Ānanda Bodhendra Sarasvatī, the disciple of Gaṅgādharendra wrote his *Tātparaya Ṭikā* on *Yogavāsiṣṭha.* Gaṅgādharendra wrote two *Bhāṣyas* on it. Mādhava Sarasvatī attempted *Pada Candrikā* commentary on this work.

Yogavāsiṣṭha is composed of several *Upākhyānas* which mainly contributed to its vast size. There are 53 important *Upākhyānas* in this work. They are as under:

1. The story of *Yogavāsiṣṭha*
2. The conversation between Rāma and Vasiṣṭha.
3. The story of Śuka
4. Vasiṣṭha's story of Origin and acquisition of knowledge.
5. The story of *Ākāśaja*
6. The story of Līlā.

7. The story of Karkaṭī Rākṣasī.
8. The story of the sons of Indu Brāhmaṇa.
9. The story of Ahalyā and Indra.
10. The story of *Citta.*
11. The story of Bala.
12. The story of *Indrajāla.*
13. *The story of Śukra.*
14. The story of Dāma, Vyāla and Kaṭa.
15. The story of Bhīma, Bhāsa and Dṛḍha.
16. The story of Daśūra.
17. Kacgītā.
18. The story of Janaka's attaining Jivanmukti.
19. The story of Puṇya and Pāvana.
20. The story of Bali.
21. The story of Prahalāda.
22. The story of Gādhī
23. The story of Uddālaka
24. The story of Suraghu
25. The story of Vītahavya
26. The story of Kāk Bhuśuṇḍa
27. The story of Queen Cuḍālā and Śikhidhvaja
28. The story of Iśvara
29. The story of Arjuna
30. The story of Śatarudra.
31. The story of Vetāla
32. The story of Bhāgīratha
33. The story of Rānī Cūḍālā

34. The story of Kirāta
35. The story of Maṇikāc
36. The story of Hastika
37. The story of Kaca
38. The story of lkṣvāku
39. The story of A Muni Settled In Turyāvasthā
40. The story of Vidyādhara
41. The story of Indra
42. The story of Maṅkī
43. The story of Manohariṇa
44. The story of Paṣāṇa
45. The story of Vipaścit
46. The story of Vaṭadhānā princes
47. The story of Śava
48. The story of Śilā
49. The story of Brahmāṇḍa
50. The story of Aindava
51. The story of Bilva
52. The story of Tāpasa
53. Kāṣṭhavaivadhika

Yogavāsiṣṭha, in fact, is the compilation of discourses delivered by the great sage Vasiṣṭha to Ram at the time of his coronation on the throne of Ayodhyā. Taking this opportunity of historic occasion, Vasiṣṭha, as per tradition, delivered his sermons on varied topics dealing with spirituality, origin of cosmos and human beings, attainment of *Mokṣa* through *Yoga* and *Samādhī*. The present treatise is bulkier in size and shape than *Rāmāyaṇa*. It sheds an ample good light on the time period of Rāma, social customs and Vedic rituals prevalent by then. It also helps unravel the mysteries of creation, decreation and *Avatāras.* It helps in ascertaining the geographical limits, i.e. longitudes and latitudes of various places during that period. Ṛṣi Vālmīki is the author of this earliest great work on *Yoga.*

Monier Williams in his work on Indian wisdom (P.370) took notice of this work as under:

> "There is a remarkable work called *Vāsiṣṭha Rāmāyaṇa* or *Yoga Vāsiṣṭha* or *Vāsiṣṭha Mahārāmāyaṇa* in the form of an exhortation, with illustrative narratives addressed by Vasiṣṭha to his pupil, the youthful Rāma, on the best means of attaining true happiness, and considered to have been composed as an appendage to the *Rāmāyaṇa* by Ṛṣi Vālmīki himself. There is another work of the same nature called the *Adhyātma Rāmāyaṇa* which is attributed to Vyāsa and treat of the moral and theological subjects connected with the life and acts of the great hero of Indian history. Many other works are extant in the vernacular dialects having the same theme for their subjects which it is needless to notice in this place".

Vasiṣṭha known as the wisest of sages, puts forth in the first part the great question of the vanity of the world, which is shown synthetically to a great length from the state of all living existences, the instinct, inclinations and passions of men, the nature of their aims and objects, with some discussions about destiny, necessity, activity and the state of the Ātmā and Paramātmā. The second part embraces various directions for the union of the Ātmā with Paramātmā (Nirguṇa Brahm), the subjective, the objective truth and the common topics of *Yoga* philosophy.

Philosophy of Yogavāsiṣṭha

Philosophy of *Yogavāsiṣṭha* pertains to Tretā yuga. It talks about Paramātmā which is self luminous and everlasting, omnipresent and supereminent.

आत्माप्रकाशरूपो हि नित्यः सर्वगतो विभुः । 6/1.29.64
ātmāprakāśarūpo hi nityaḥ sarvagato vighuḥ
Ātmā is self luminous, everlasting, omnipresent and superrminent.

But the soul is self-luminous, everlasting, omnipresent and supereminent.

Second element discussed in detail is citta. Citta embodied Ātmā overpowered by manas. It may also be known as manas based awareness. It is deceptive and individuated element. It pertains to heart.

चित्तं शठमहंकारं विद्धिहार्दं बृहत्तमः। 6/1.29.64

cittaṁ śaṭham ahaṁkāraṁ viddhi hardaṁ bṛgattamaḥ

[Meaning] The mind is deceptive and the ego is situated in the heart with too much pride and vanity.

Manas is also described like demon who has taken possession of the empty house of the body and has like an evil spirit, silenced and overpowered upon intangible citta in it.

पिशाचोऽपि मनो राम शून्यदेहगृहे स्थितः
भावयत्येष दुष्टात्मा मौनमुत्तम संस्पृशन्।। 6/1.29.66

piśāco'pi mano rāma śūnyadehagṛhe sthitaḥ
bhāvayattyeṣa duṣṭātmā maunam uttam sanspṛśan

[Meaning] The manas, like a demon, has also taken possession of the empty house of the body. Like an evil spirit, the manas has silenced and overpowered the intangible citta in it.

Third element discussed is the corporeal body formed of five physical elements of *Prakṛti.* In fact, this physical body is the basis or dwelling place of Ātmā often overpowered by the demon of mind. This dwelling of the body, according to *Yogavāsiṣṭha*, has the bones for its posts and the blood and flesh for its mortar and the nine holes for many windows. At the question as to who formed this body, *Yogavāsiṣṭha* replies that no one forms this body.

अस्थिस्थूणं नवद्वारं रक्तमांसावलेपनम्।
शरीरसदनं राम न केनचिदिदं कृतम्।। 6/1.28.12

asthisthūṇaṁ navadvāraṁ raktamānsāvalepanam
śarīrasadanaṁ rāma na kenacididaṁ kṛtam

[Meaning] This dwelling of the body that has bones for its posts, blood and flesh for its mortar, and the nine holes for so many windows, is built by no one.

But it is the manifestation of our willed decision.

संकल्पनिर्माणदेहा सहस्रशः ।

sankalpanirmāṇ dehā sahasraśaḥ

[Meaning] These thousands of bodies are not built by anyone, but caused by the willed decision of the individuals dwelling in them

So long as we wish to live, we are dragged into corporeal body. If we cease to long for life, our emancipation becomes easy.

What is Manas ?

This question has often vexed the scholiasts and psychologists. While discussing the subject of the origin of the human body and citta (Chapter 91), the thinking power or conscious mind has been perceived in *Yogavāsiṣṭha* as the cause of all things in course of time, and the source of all its pleasurable and painful feelings, which develop and diminish in itself and never grow without it.

अविनाभाविनीनित्यं काल कांक्षिक्रमे तथा ।
सर्वमुत्पादयत्येतच्चित्तकः संविदात्मकः ।। 5.91.51

avinābhāvinī nityaṁ kāla kāṅkṣikrame tathā
sarvam utpādayatyetchchittakaḥ saṁvidātmakaḥ

[Meaning] The conscious mind is the cause of all things in the course of time and the source of all its pleasure and pain which rise and fall in itself and never grow without it.

At the same time concept of sensation and citta has also been defined as the union of the breath of life with the organs and if this union is united with desire, origin of citta takes place.

यथा प्राणेन्द्रियानन्दमानन्दपवनावुभौ ।
चित्तस्योत्पादिके सार्धं यदैत वासने तदा ।। 5.91.52

yathā prāṇendriyānandamānanda pavanāvubhau
chittasyotpādike sārdhaṁ yadaita vāsane tadā

[Meaning] As the union of the breath of life with the organs produces sensations, so these being united with desire are productive of the citta.

This is why the living and sensitive plants which are devoid of desire are devoid of citta also.

In this course, it may be stated that end of desire, is the end of citta and end of citta tantamount to the end of birth-death cycle which is known in philosophical terms emancipation.

Difference between Citta and Sensations

The union of breath and the organs that produce sensation. But when sense organs are united with desire, they produce citta. This way living and sensitive plants or living beings which are devoid of desire are also devoid of citta or *manomayakoṣa.*

यथा प्राणेन्द्रियानन्दमानन्दपवनावुभौ ।
चित्तस्योत्पादिके सार्धं यदैते वासने तदा ।। 5.91.52

yathā prāṇendriyānandamānanda pavanāvubhau
chittasyotpādike sārdhaṁ yadaita vāsane tadā

[Meaning] As the union of the breath of life with the organs produces sensations, so these being united with desire are productive of the citta.

Relationship of thought and vital air

Yogavāsiṣtha establishes keen relationship between thought and vital air. Accordingly:

संशान्ते पवनस्पन्दे यथा पांसुर्नभस्तले ।
यः प्राणपवनस्पन्दभित्तस्पन्दः स एव हि ।। 5.92.31

saṁśānte pavanspande yathā pansurnabhastale
yaḥ prāṇapavanaspandabhittaspandaḥ sa eva hi

[Meaning] As flying dust sets on the ground after a gust of wind passes, so the flying thoughts of the mind are stopped when our breathings are put to a stop, they being the one and the same thing.

As the flying dust is set on the ground, after the gust of the wind is over, so flying thoughts of the wind are stopped, when our breathings are put to rest.

In fact there is ultimate connection between thought and vital air. The author of *Yogavāsiṣtha* says, 'Thought commences and corresponds with vital respiration. A long thought draws a long breath and a quick one is attended with a rapid vibration of breath".

Reflection on customs

The study of *Yogavāsiṣṭha* gives sometimes an interesting insight into the old customs. Today we think that the custom of shaking hands both on meeting and parting is conspicuous to modern days and especially seem to have been borrowed from westerns. But *Yogavāsiṣṭha* tells us that this was an age old custom prevalent in the country. The following reference of *Yogavāsiṣṭha* is worth noting in this regard :

व्योम्नि योजनामात्रां तु मदनुव्रज्यया गतः ।
करं करेणावष्टभ्य बलात्संरोधिः खगः ।। 6/1.27.14

vyomni yojanāmātrāṁ tu madnuvrajyayā gataḥ
karaṁ kareṇāvaṣṭabhya balātsanrodhiḥ khagaḥ

[Meaning] That is the Khaga (Kāka) followed me a few miles (*yojana*) in the air, when I compelled him to return after shaking hands'.

Prohibition of idol worship

On the question of worship of the Paramātmā, the *Yogavāsiṣt ha* is very much clear. According to it, Paramātmā is of the nature of Jñāna.

आत्मसंवित्तिरूपम् – 6/1.29.129

ātmasaṁvittirūpam

So, the worship of Paramātmā can be done through accumulation of Jñāna and by forsaking the adoration of idols. Those that are devoted to any form of fictitious cult or idol worship, are subject to endless misery.

आत्मसंवित्तिरूपं तु त्यक्त्वा देवार्चनं जनाः ।
कृत्रिमार्चासु ये सक्ताश्चिरं क्लेशं□भजन्ति ते ।। 6/1.29.129

In fact the idol worshippers have been compared with little children playing with their dolls.

बालक्रीडोपमं च ते अध्यात्मध्यानादृते ब्रह्मकुर्वन्तो
देवपूजनम् । 6/1.29.130

On the question of as to what is the best method of the worship of Brahma, the treatise further maintains that Brahma should be worshipped by accumulation of knowledge.

ज्ञानार्जनेनाविरतं पूजनीयः स सर्वदा – 6/1.29.131

True *pūjā* is considered to be the meditation of pure Paramātmā (Brahma) and not otherwise, since the Brahma is the intelligent and everlasting.

त्वमेतच्चेतनाकाशमात्मानं जीवमव्ययम्।
स्वभावं विद्धि न त्वन्यः पूज्यः पूजात्मपूजनम्।। 6/1.29.132

Paramātmā is not to be worshipped with the help of external means like flowers and frankincense.

अबहिः साधनासाध्यम् – 30.31

Yogavāsiṣṭha also discards the concept of worship of mere natural and use of flowers and incense sticks in worship.

नातिदेवार्चने योग्यः पुष्पधूपचयो महान्। 6/1.30.4

Yogavāsiṣṭha, describes the act of idol worship as unlearned, simple as those of children and childish.

अव्युत्पन्नधियो ये हि बालपेलवचेतसः।
कृत्रिमार्चामयं तेषां देवार्चनमुदाहृत्तम्।। 6/1.30.5

In fact, it is due only to lack of understanding that a person worships with flowers, etc. and attribute the Paramātmā to false images of their own making.

शमवोधद्यभावे हि पुष्पाद्यैर्वार्चयन्ति हि।
मिथ्यैव कल्पितैरेतमाकारे कल्पितात्मके।। 6/1.30.6

Yogavāsiṣṭha unleashes scathing attacks on idols as to how the idols may be called as gods, who having their hands and feet, are yet devoid of their consciousness which is the pith of body.

पादपाण्यादिमानन्यो यो वा देवः प्रकल्प्यते।
संविन्मात्रादृते ब्रह्मन्किसार किल कथ्यताम्।। 6/1.30.19

Mysteries of creation

Several mysteries of creation have been unfolded in the *Yogavāsiṣṭha. Yogavāsiṣṭha* also unravels the secrets of creation. While shedding light on the nature of internal and external relations, it says that Brahmā took the period of one *Mahākalpa* to create this universe.

महाकल्प समाधान चिरकल्पित कल्पनम्।
वन्द्य संसक्तिवशतो ब्राह्मं स्फुरति वै वपुः।।

mahākalpa samādhā cirkalpita kalpanam
vandya sansaktivaśato brāhmaṁ sphurati vai vapuḥ

[Meaning] This long back created universe took one kalpa for its creation.Salute worthy body of Brahma becomes manifest during this period.

Thus according to *Yogavāsiṣṭha*, the whole creation accomplished not in seconds, but it took the period of Mahākalpa for its completion.

Mystery of *Kūrmāvatāra*

Yogavāsiṣṭha while giving an account of past ages clarifies that *Kūrmāvatāra* is the resurrection of earth from waters and accordingly, the earth has sunk into water five times and lifted up as many times by the divine *Kūrmāvatāra* of Viṣṇu from below the overflowing ocean.

अन्तर्धानगता धात्री वारपंचकमुद्धता।
मुने पंचसु सर्गेषु कूर्मेणैव पयोनिधेः।। 6/1.22.12

antardhāna-gatā dhātrī vārapañchakam uddhatā
mune pañcasu sargeṣu kūrmeṇaiva payonidheḥ

[Meaning] I saw the earth sinking five times under, and lifted up as many times from the ocean by the divine Kurma Manvantara, the incarnation of Vishnu in the form of the tortoise.

Definition of *Manvantara*

While relating to the account of past ages, *Yogavāsiṣṭha* goes to define *Manvantara* as the measurement of time. Accordingly, *Manvantara* is a symbol of reversal of the course of world. With every *Manvantara* in fray, reversal of the course of the world takes place.

प्रतिमन्वन्तरं ब्रह्मन्विपर्यस्ते जगत्क्रमे।
संनिवेशेऽन्यथा जाते प्रयाते संश्रुते जने।। 6/1.22.37

pratimanvantaraṁ brahmanviparyaste jagatkrame
sanveśe'nyathā jāte prayāte sanśrute jane.

[Meaning] O Brahmin, every *manvantara* is attended with a reversion in the course of our universe. The polarity of earth changes and a new generation is born to supplant the old men of renown.

In the process of reversal, the polarity of *Meru* is changed, the points of compass are altered, the difference in the sides of quarters takes place and so nothing remains as positive truth except our conception of it.

संस्थानमन्यथा तस्मिन्स्थिते यान्ति दिशोऽन्यथा।
न सन्नासज्जगन्मन्ये भ्रमयन्केवलं धियः।। 6/1.22.47

sansthānamanyathā tasminsthite yānti diśo'nyathā
na sannāsajjaganmanye bhramyankevalaṁ dhiyaḥ

[Meaning] The site of the polar circle of Meru and the course of the planets being changed in different directions, there follows an alteration of the points of the compass and a difference in the sides of the quarters. Therefore there is nothing as a positive truth except our conception of it as such and such.

In the preceding lines it has been laid down that during the process of this type of reversal in a *Manvantara* north goes to other side and Meru also shifts its side.

दिगुत्तराभूदन्येयं पूर्वमेव महीधरः। 6/1.22.45

diguttarābhūdanyeyaṁ pūrvameva mahidharaḥ

[Meaning] Then the north was on another side and yet this Meru was in another place.

This reversal is said to have effected the change in the lodgings of the animate beings on the earth and as such the lodgings also shift sometimes to Vidhayan part of continents, sometimes to the Kaccha part and sometimes to the Sahya or Dardura parts of continents. It is shifted sometimes to glaciated part of continents and sometimes to Malaya part.

कदाचिदहमेकान्ते विन्ध्यकच्छकृतालयः ।
कदाचित्सह्यनिलयः कदाचिद्दर्दुरालयः ।। 6/1.22.39
कदाचिद् हिमवद्वासी कदाचिन्मलयाचलः ।
कदाचित् प्राक्तनेनैव संनिवेशेन भूधरम् ।। 6/1.22.40

kadācidahmekānte vindhyakachchhkṛtālayaḥ
kadācitsahyanilaya kadācidddardurālayaḥ.
kadācid himvadvāsī kadācinmalayācalaḥ
kadācit prāktanenaiva sanivesена bhūdharam

[Meaning] Sometimes I had to remain in my solitary retreat by the side of the Vindhya range, and sometimes on the ridge of Sahya Mountain. At other times I had my residence on the Dardura Hills, so my lodging is ever shifting from one place to another and never fixed in any spot forever.

I often have been a resident of the Himalayas, of Malaya Mountain in the south of India, then led by destiny, as I described before, I found my last abode on this Mount Meru.

What is Meru?

According to *Yogavāsiṣṭha* Meru is not a mountain, but the surface of the earth or say lithosphere is called Meru.

मेरुर्भूपीठः

merurbhūpīṭhaḥ

[Meaning] Lithospher of earth is called Meru.

At another place, Meru is used as an attributive of earth, which stands to mean earth qualified by meru or maru or sand.

मेरुर्धरा–5.41.31

merurdharā

[Meaning] This earth is meru

Thus Meru is symbolic of lithosphere and not of mountain.

Situation of Plakṣa Dvīpa

As per description of *Yogavāsiṣṭha* Plakṣa Dvīpa was encircled by the snowy plains of Himalayas.

ततो गोमेदकद्वीप लेखयैवं प्रमाणया।
इक्ष्वब्धि लेखयाप्येवं हिमवद्सानु शुद्धया। 3.25.22

tato gomedakadvīpa lekhayaivaṁ pramāṇayā
ikṣvabdhi lekhayāpyevaṁ himvadsānu śuddhayā.

[Meaning] Thereafter stretches Plaksa continent, double the size of the former and surrounded by the belt of the sea of sugar that appears like the snowy plains of Himalaya.

Shape of Earth as looked from sky

The earth appeared as a lotus in the heart of Brahmāṇḍa Puruṣa, the eight sides forming the petals of the flower, the clouds being its pistils and the pericarp containing its sweet flavour.

ब्रह्माण्डनर ह्मद्मर्हिगष्टकदलवृहत्।
गिरिकेसर संबाधस्वामोदभरसुंदरम्।। 3.25.2

brahmāṇḍanara hṛmdmarhigaṣṭakadalavṛhat
girikesara saṁbādhasvāmodabharasundaram.

[Meaning] They saw the world appearing like a lotus in the heart of Nara (the primeval Man or eternal Spirit pervading the universe). Its eight sides form the flower petals, the hills its pistils, and the center contains its sweet flavor.

The earth like a lotus is situated on the surface of waters of oceans.

कदाचिदास्यदामोधिकपंकपितदिग्दलम्।
अधोनालगतानतदैत्यदानवकंटकम्।। 3.25.6

kadācidāsyadāmodhikapaṅkapitadigdalam
adhonālagatānatadaitya-dānava-kaṅṭakam.

1[Meaning] The earth, like a lotus, is situated on the surface of the waters of the ocean. At times the motion of the ocean makes the earth shake causing earthquakes. The earth rests upon the serpent Sesha as its support, and is girt about by demons as its thorns and prickles.

Jambudvīpa

Jambudvīpa was the name of highly populated region according to *Yogavāsiṣṭha.*

लक्षयोजन विस्तीर्णानाकीर्णांचिरजो लबैः।
नानाजनपदव्यूहस्थिरावश्याय सीकराम्।। 3.25.13

lakṣayojana vistīrṇānākīrṇāchirjo labaiḥ
nānājanapadvyūhasthirāvaśyāya sīkarām

[Meaning] It stretches a million miles with more land than water. Its habitable parts are as thick as frozen ice in winter.

स्थलेष्वामंडलांतस्थ जनजालालिमंडलाम् – 3.25.10

sthaleṣvāmaṇḍalāntastha janajālālimaṇḍalām

[Meaning] Its lakes are like dewdrops on a lotus leaf, and its forests are like the flower's pollen. The people inhabiting the land all around are like a swarm of bees.

Kalpa Tree

The description of Kalpa tree as is available from *Yogavāsiṣṭ ha* gives one to understand (in spiritual sense) a tree of desire which branches out into various objects of our wish. Its flowers are all sanguine hopes and expectations which are hidden under the dark mist of futurity. The crown dwelling in its dark hollow, is the indwelling obscure Ātmā, which is hidden under the imperious gloom of our ignorant minds and false egotism. Its nest is in the highest divinity and it is immortal because it is a particle or Eternal spirit.

पुष्परेण्वभ्रवलितं रत्नस्तबकदन्तुरम्।
उत्सेधनिर्जिताकाशं शृंगे शृंगमिवार्पितम्। 6/1.15.2

puṣpareṇvabhravalitaṁ ratnastabakadanturam.
utsedhanirjitākāśaṁ śṛṅge śṛṅgamivārpitam.

[Meaning] This tree was covered with the pollen of its flowers which shrouded it like a thick mist or cloud. Its flowers shown as bright as brilliant gems. Its great height reaching the sky made it look like a steeple standing upon the peak.

Its equivalent, in astronomical sense, is the sky with stars as its flowers, clouds as its leaves, flashes of lighting as its filaments circumvent beams of the radiant sun as the pollen of its flowers.

ताराद्विगुणपुष्पौघं मेघद्विगण पल्लवम् ।
रश्मिद्विगुण रेण्वभ्रं तडिद्द्विगुणमंजरीम् – 6 / 1.15.3

tārādviguṇa-puṣpaughaṁ meghadviguṇa pallavam
raśmidviguṇa reṇvabhraṁ taḍiddviguṇa-mañjarīm.

[Meaning] Its flowers were twice as many as the stars in heaven, and its leaves doubled the clouds in their bulk and thickness. Its filaments were more shiny than flashes of lightning, and its flower pollen was far brighter than the surrounding sunbeams.

Purāṇas undergo interpolations

It has been made clear in the *Yogavāsiṣṭha* while recounting the past ages that *Purāṇas*, though agreeing in the main substance, are also full of interpolations, that they have been greatly multiplied in successive ages or *yugas.*

एकार्थानि समग्राणि बहुपाठानि मेऽनघ ।
पुराणानि प्रवर्तन्ते प्रसृतानि युगंप्रति ।। 6 / 1.22.20

ekārthāni samagrāṇi bahupāṭhāni me'nagha
purāṇāni pravartante prasṛtāni yugaṁ prati.

[Meaning] O evil free saint, the Puranas, though they agree in the main substance, are greatly multiplied in successive ages.

Varied Readings and rituals of the Vedas

In the *Yogavāsiṣṭha*, it has been clarified that Vedas were subjected to various readings, as well as rituals from age to age, likewise the differences in the intellects of the scholars occurred from age to age. Vedas though remained intact so far as their internal structure was concerned but were subjected to various readings and rituals in various schools that emerged from time to time.

युगं प्रति धियां पुंसां न्यूनाधिकतया मुने ।
क्रियांगपाठवैचित्र्ययुक्तान्वेदान्स्मराम्यहम् ।। 6 / 1.22.19

yugaṁ prati dhiyā puṁsā nyūnādhikatayā mune
kriyāṅgapāṭha-vaicitryyuktānvedānsmarāmyaham.

[meaning] I remember, O silent sage, the difference in the intellects of men at every succeeding age and the various readings of Vedas and various ritual observances of mankind.

Period of Rāma

Yogavāsiṣtha also supplies the information regarding the time period of Rāma. In this connection following *śloka* may be referred to

अद्य राम कृते क्षीणे त्रेता सम्प्रति वर्तते – 6/1.27.18

adya rāma kṛte kṣīṇe tretā samprati vartate.

[Meaning] Now, O Rama, that Satya yuga has gone by and we are in the middle of the *treta yuga* when you are born to subdue your enemies.

From the above statement it is clear that during Rāma's time *Satyayuga* had elapsed and *Tretā* was in currency. According to the information of Mahābhārata Rāma was was born in the sandhi period of Dvāpara and Tretayuga.The concerned verse reads like this:

संधौ तु समनुप्राप्ते त्रेताया द्वापरस्य च
रामो दाशरथिर्भूत्वा भविष्यामि जगत्पति।। Sānti Parva, (348.19)

sandhau tu samanuprāpte tretāyā dvāparasya ca
rāmo dāśarathirbhūtvā bhaviṣyā jagatpati.

[Meaning] During the transition period of tretā and dvāpara Daśaratha's son Rāma will be born ho will become the emperor of the whole world.

Presently 28th Kaliyuga is in currency. As such the 28th Tretāyuga has passed.

However Puranic sources give a more specific information. Accordingly Rāma was born in the 24th Tretāyuga. The references to this effect can be quoted as under.

त्रेतायुगे चतुर्विंशे रावणः तपसः क्षयात् ।
रामं दाशरथिं प्राप्त सगणः क्षयमीयीवान् ।। Vāyu Purāṇa, 70-88
tretāyuge caturviṁśe rāvaṇaḥ tapasaḥ kṣayāt
rāmaṁ dāśarathiṁ prāpta sagaṇaḥ kṣayamīyīvān.

[Meaning] In the 24th Tretāyuga Rāvaṇa alongwith his family members will invite his destruction at the hands of Rāma, due to the reduction of the fruits of his penances .

चतुर्विंशे युगे वत्स त्रेतायां रघुवंशजः।
रामो नाम भविष्यामि चतुर्व्यूहः सनातनः।। Brahmāṇḍa Purāṇa, 22.36.3

chaturvimśe yuge vatsa tretāyāṁ raghuvaṁśajaḥ
rāmo nāma bhaviṣyāmi chaturvyūha sanātanaḥ.

[Meaning] In the 24th Tretāyuga, Rāma will be born in the lineage of Raghus. He will lead the four fold army.

चतुर्विंशे युगे चापि विश्वामित्रपुरःसरः।
लोके राम इति ख्यातः तेजसा भास्करोपमः।Harivaṁśa Purāṇa, 22.104

chaturviṁśe yuge cāpi viśvāmitrapuraḥsaraḥ
loke rāma iti khyātaḥ tejasā bhāskaropamaḥ.

[Meaning] In the 24th Tretāyuga, Rāma led by Viśvāmitra will become famous due to his effulgence like sun.

24th Tretā yuga works out, given astronomical calculations, to be around 18 Million years. The calculations are as under:

Years of 28th Kaliyuga elapsed	=5116
Years of 28th Dvāpara elapsed	=8,40,000
Years of 28th Tretā elapsed	=1296000
Years of 28th Satyayuga elapsed	=1728000
Years of 27th Mahāyuga elapsed	=4320000
Years of 26th Mahāyuga elapsed	=4320000
Years of 25th Mahāyuga elapsed	=4320000
Years of 24th Kaliyuga elapsed	=432000
Years of 24th Dvāpara elapsed	=8,40,000
Years of Sandhi of Dvāpara and Tretā	=108000

Total years elapsed	= 18209116

We have some more specific astronomical information about the birth of Rāma. Accordingly during the birth of Rāma vernal equinox used to take place in Punarvasu constellations. Presently vernal equinox takes place in Pūrva Bhādrapada constellations which has a precession of 117^0. It takes 117x 72= 8424 years for the precession of 117^0. As such nearest occurrence of vernal equinox in Punarvasu constellations comes about to be 6409 BC or Dvāpara 862693. The same cycle of vernal equinox to take place in Punarvasu constellations is repeated every 25920 years. From Dvāpara 862693 to the sandhi of 24th Tretā and Dvāpara, 702 precession cyles completes and the time period of Rāma in 24th Tretāyuga comes about 1818180 years ago. As such, period of Rāma as per Indian chronology 18 million years ago.[i] It is also mentioned in Purāṇas that by Rāma's time last phase of Himalayan upliftment was also over. The above fact is corroborated by the internal evidence of Rāmāyaṇa and archeoloigcal findings. In Vālmīki Ramāyaṇa (Dr. Ravi Prakash Arya, 1998)[ii], Sundara Kāṇḍa (4.28), it is mentioned that when Hanumāna first reached Rāvana's palace, he saw decked gateways surrounded by four tusked elephants resembling the masses of white clouds and wild beasts and birds. The verse goes like this:

वारणैश्च चतुर्दन्तैः श्वेताभ्रनिचयोपमैः ।

भूषितैः रुचिरद्वारं मत्तैश्च मृगपक्षिभिः ।।

vāraṇaiśca chaturdantaiḥ śvetābhranicayopamaiḥ
bhūṣitaiḥ ruciradvāraṁ mattaiśca mṛgapakṣibhiḥ.

[Meaning] The inner apartments of Rāvaṇa were adorned with elephants, fourtusked elephants resembling masses of white clouds; and possessing graceful gateways alongwith deers and chirping birds.

At another place (Rāmāyaṇa, Sundara kāṇḍa, 27.12), Trijaṭā, a Rākṣasī, sees in her dream illustrious Rāma and Lakṣamaṇa mounted on huge elephant with four tusks and resembling a hill. The original verse reads as under:

राघवश्च पुनर्दृष्टश्चतुर्दन्त महागजम् ।

आरूढः शैलसंकाशं चकास सहलक्ष्मणः ।।

rāghavaśca punardṛṣṭaśchaturdanta mahāgajam
ārūḍha śailasaṅkāśaṁ chakāsa sahalakṣamaṇaḥ

[Meaning] I saw again Lakṣamaṇa appear in effulgence, seated on a huge elephant, having four tusks and resembling a bull.

Mention of four tusked elephants by Ṛṣi Vālmīki is a glaring evidence of the fact that elephants with four tusks must have been present during the period of Rāmāyaṇa and Ṛṣi Vālmīki. The Encarta Encyclopedia informs us about the presence of four-tusked elephants on earth between 38 million years ago to 15 million years ago. They are named as Mastodontoidea. Accordingly, Mastodontoidea evolved around 38 million years ago and became extinct about 15 million years ago when the shaggy and two tusked Mastodons increased in population.

The above proof lends a strong support to the authenticity of tradition of Purānas. Now one may easily understand that the astronomical time calculation system adopted by Vedic seers is only the key to the true chronology of India history. Whatever said or done in the name of modern calculations is quite misleading and proof of their misunderstanding of the Indian knowledge system.

Four tusked elephant of Rāmāyaṇa

Similes in *Yogavāsiṣṭha*

We have heard a lot about the similes of Kālidāsa, but the similes of *Yogavāsiṣṭha* are no less remarkable even while elucidating the philosophical imports. To illustrate, one may quote here an example of impurity of heart being equated with the impurity of Gold.

कलंकयन्तः कलंकेन प्रोच्यते हेम नान्यथा।
भावासक्त्य समासक्त उक्तो जन्तुर्हि नान्यथा। 5.74.70

kalaṅkayantaḥ kalaṅkena prochyate hema nānyathā
bhāvāsaktya samāsakta ukto janturhi nānyathā

[Meaning] The gold becomes impure by its inward alloy, and not by its outward soil; so a man becomes unholy by the impurity of heart and foulness of his mind and not on account of dust or dirt on his body.

Authorship and date

The authorship of this great work is assigned to sage Valmīki, the famous author of Rāmāyaṇa. The *Viṣṇudharmottara Purāṇa* says that Vālmiki was born in the *Tretāyuga* as a form of Viṣṇu who composed the Rāmāyaṇa, and that people desirious of earning knowledge should worship Vālmiki[1]. He was contemporary to Rāma and the date of Rāma may also be the date of Vālmīki. This way Vālmīk's time may also be calculated minimum 900 thousand years ago and maximum 18 million years ago.

Yogavāsiṣṭha was composed by Ṛṣi Vālmīki after the composition of Rāmāyana was over. So the time period of first original composition Yogavāsiṣṭha by Vālmīki was also 900 thousands year (as per 28th Tretā) or 18 million years (as per 24th Tretā) ago. Present edition has reached us through thousand years long tradition.

---

1 Mythology of Vishnu and His Incarnations by Manohar Laxman Varadpande (2009), p. 166

Divinizing of Human Being

In India, philosophy has never been an intellectual pursuit of knowledge of Ultimate Reality. The task of a philosopher here is not over with the construction of a metaphysical system which satisfies the intellect. The chief concern of human life is permanent abolition of suffering and restlessness which is common characteristics of human beings. The Saṅkhya philosopher says:

त्रिविधदुःखस्यात्यन्तनिवृत्तिरत्यन्तपुरुषार्थः
trividhadukhasya atyanta nivṛttir atyanta puruṣārthaḥ

[Meaning] The permanent abolition of three types of suffering arising from three factors metaphysical, astrophysical and physical is the chief concern of human life.

The above phenomenon is beautifully depicted in Yogavāsiṣṭ ha. "All creatures", says the author of *Yogavāsiṣṭha* (6/1.108.20), "strive to be happy,"

आनन्दायैव भूतानि यतन्ते यानि कानिचित्।

[Meaning] Oh! Happiness is the end and aim of all beings on the earth.

But hardly any one of them found happy in the world. "The world is full of misery and suffering in all directions"

कास्तादृशो यासु न सन्ति दोषाः।
कास्तादिशो यासु न दुःखदाह।।
कास्ताः प्रजा यासु न भंगुरत्वम्।
कास्ताः क्रिया यासु न नाम माया।। योगवासिष्ठ, 1.27.31

[Meaning] What is that thing in the world, which has no fault in it; and what is that which does not afflict or grieve us; what being is born that is not subjected to death, and what are those acts that are free from deceit.

Simultaneously, it is stated that cause of all suffering is

rooted in the ignorance of real nature of Self, the world and their relation. It does not affect the wise man who knows that is worth knowing and who has attained the right outlook.

प्राज्ञं विज्ञातविज्ञेयं सम्यग्दर्शनमाधयः।
न दहन्ति वनं वर्षासिक्तमग्निशिखा इव। योगवासिष्ठ, 2.11.41

[Meaning] But the troubles of this world cannot afflict the wise man, who knows the knowable, and discerns all things (in their true light); just as it is impossible for the flame of fire to burn down a wood drenched by the rains.

The root of suffering is cut off by the self-realization.

सर्वदुःखशिरश्छेद आत्मालोकेन जायते। योगवासिष्ठ, 5.75.46

[Meaning] Realization of the soul (self realization) is sure to cut off all pains and pangs of the world from their root.

Ignorance of Self is the source of all troubles and the realization of it is that of permanent bliss and peace.

हे जना अपरिज्ञात आत्मा वो दुःखसिद्धये।
परिज्ञातस्त्वनन्ताय सुखायोपशमाय च।। योगवासिष्ठ, 5.5.23

[Meaning] O you men that are unacquainted with the divine spirit, you bear your souls for misery alone; but realizing the spirit you become entitled to eternal happiness and tranquility.

One may rule over the entire world, yet one will not attain peace unless one realizes the Self.

करोतु भुवने राज्यं विशत्वम्भोदमम्बु वा।
नात्मलाभादृते जन्तुर्विश्रान्तिमधिगच्छति।। योगवासिष्ठ, 4.57.34

[Meaning] A man may rule the whole world, or he may pierce through the clouds and interfere in heaven by his yoga; yet he cannot enjoy the solace of his soul without his realization of it.

The Vedic philosopher describes the main goal of human life as achievement of dharma, artha, kāma and mokṣa. While achieving the goal of dharma, artha and kāma, one has to pass through sufferings and restlessness. However, the achievement of mokṣa makes a seeker relieved of his suffering and restlessness. Divinization is the only qualification for seeking Mokṣa. The divinization cannot be achieved through the information (knowledge) of God (jñāna) alone; rather it can be achieved through the realization of God (vijñāna). Mere information is called as jñāna and realization of it becomes vijñāna. Ādi Shankar observes:

ज्ञानं विषय विषयानुभूतिविज्ञानम्। विज्ञानमानन्दं ब्रह्म।

jñānaṁ viṣaya viṣyānubhūtir vijñānam. Vijñānaṁ ānandaṁ brahma.

[Meaning] Mere information is Jñāna. Realization of it is vijāna. When the Brahma is realized, one gets rid of all sufferings and becomes blissful.

According to Yogavāsiṣṭha, divinization can be achieved only through right knowledge and not through rigour of rituals, penances, devotion and worships of personal Gods and retiring into forest.

Here we shall have a bird's eye view of the means of Self realization as depicted in the Yogavāsiṣṭha.

What is the nature of Self?: What then is the nature of Self, realization of which brings to an end of all sufferings of individuals? This issue has been hotly debated in the Śāstras. According to Yogavāsiṣṭha, there are four views about the Self, current among men of various level of knowledge, the fourth of which is the right view that must be realized in order to be really happy.

The first view describes Self as the body.

आपादमस्तकमहं मातापितृविनिर्मितः।
इत्येको निश्चयो राम बन्धायसद्विलोकनात्।। योगवासिष्ठ, 5.17.14

[Meaning] He who considers his whole body (from head to feet) as biological inheritance from his parents (devoid of spiritual part) is surely born to the bondage of the world. (This is first kind of view).

देहोऽहमिति तां विद्धि दुःखायैव न शान्तये। योगवासिष्ठ, 5.73.11

[Meaning] The view that 'I am only body' leads one to misery and not to solace.

The second view describes Self as the mind based

consciousness (chitta).

स्वसंकल्पमयाकारं यावत्संसारभावि यत्।
चित्तं तद्विद्धि जीवस्य रूपं रामातिवाहिकम्।।

योगवासिष्ठ, 6/1.124.19

[Meaning] The living being had an intrinsic body also, which is derived from within; and is composed of all its wishes in the world, and is known as mind based consciousness/awareness (chitta).

The third view describes Self as the Spirit, which is beyond the body and mind and which is the subtler than even the 100th part of the tip of hair."

अतीतः सर्वभावेभ्यो वालाग्रादप्यहं तनुः।
इति द्वितीयो मोक्षाय निश्चयो जायते सताम्।। योगवासिष्ठ, 5.17.15

[Meaning] But they who are certain of their immaterial soul, which is finer than the point of a hair, are another class of men; who are called the wise and are born for their libration.

The fourth conviction describes the Self as the entire Universe existing in the state of subtle etheric voidness (śunyam vyoma-samam).

जगज्जालपदार्थात्मा सर्वमेवाहमक्षयः।
तृतीयो निश्चयेत्थमं मोक्षायैव रघूद्वह।। योगवासिष्ठ, 5.17.16
अहं जगद्वा सकलं शून्यं व्योमसमं सदा।
एवमेष चतुर्थोऽन्यो निश्चयो मोक्षसिद्धये।। योगवासिष्ठ, 5.17.17

[Meaning] There is a third class who considers themselves as same with the universal soul of the world. They are also entitled for liberation. The fourth class considers themselves as the entire universe existing in the state of subtle etheric voidness. They are surely partakers of liberation.

Such seekers upon self-realization associate themselves with everything in the Universe- the sky, the stars, the directions, the planets, all natural forces, darkness, clouds, oceans, air and fire etc.

अहंखमहमादित्यो दिशोऽहमहमप्यधः।
अहं दैत्या अहं देवा लोकाश्चाहमहं महः।। योगवासिष्ठ, 5.73.3

अहं तमोऽहमभ्राणि भूः समुद्रादिकं त्वहम्।
रजो वायुरथाग्निश्च जगत्सर्वमिदं त्वहम्।। योगवासिष्ठ, 5.73.4

[Meaning] Associate yourself with the sky, the sun, the directions, the planets, the stars, all worlds, and vastness of universe, darkness, clouds, lithosphere, hydrosphere, atom particles, air, energy and entire universe.

They perceive all that exists in the universe as their own, as the waves of an ocean are of the ocean.

यन्नाम किंचित्त्रैलोक्यं स एवावयवो मम।।
तरंगोऽब्धाविवेत्यन्तर्यः पश्यति स पश्यति।। योगवासिष्ठ, 4.22.33

[Meaning] Whatever exists in the three worlds, I perceive it as my own. As the waves in the ocean are of ocean. He seeth truly who seeth thus. (This is the right perception).

They see themselves in the fragrance of flowers; in the hue of petals and leaves, in the figure of all forms and in the perception of all perceptible.

कुसुमेष्वहमामोदः पुष्पपत्रेष्वहं छविः।
छविष्वहं रूपकला रूपेष्वनुभवोऽप्यहम्।। योगवासिष्ठ, 5.34.52

[Meaning] I see myself in the fragrance of flowers, in the hue of petals and leaves, in the figure of all forms and in the perception of all perceptible.

The real Self is pervaded by Brahman. This entire network of the expansive Universe is also pervaded by stainless Brahman.

यदिदं किंचिदाभोगि जगज्जालं प्रदृश्यते।
तत्सर्वममलं ब्रह्म भवत्येतद्व्यवस्थितम्।। योगवासिष्ठ, 6/1.11.16

[Meaning] All this visible extensive network of worlds is pervaded by stainless Brahma. It is an established view.

The Brahman is that reality from which all the beings of this Universe arise, in which they stay and into which they merge. The consciousness in which the knower, known and knowledge; perceiver, perceived and perception (i.e. subject, the object and their relation) and the agent, the action and the instrument appear and disappear. It is immense joy from which the sprays of joy are scattered on the Earth and in Heaven; and for which all creatures live.

यतः सर्वाणि भूतानि प्रतिभान्ति स्थितानि च।
यत्रैवोपशमं यान्ति तस्मै सत्यात्मने नमः।। योगवासिष्ठ, 1.1.1

[Meaning] Salutations to the Satyātmā Brahman from whom spring forth living and non-living beings, wherein they stay and merge in the end.

ज्ञाताज्ञानं तथा ज्ञेयं द्रष्टा दर्शनदृश्यभूः।
कर्त्ता हेतुः क्रिया यस्मात्तस्मै ज्ञप्त्यात्मने नमः।। योगवासिष्ठ, 1.1.2

[Meaning] Salutations to Jñanātmā Brahman from whom spring forth knower, knowledge and knowable; seer, sight and visible universe; doer, cause and action.

स्फुरन्ति सीकरा यस्मादानन्दस्याम्बरे
सर्वेषां जीवनं तस्मै ब्रह्मानन्दात्मने नमः।। योगवासिष्ठ, 1.1.3

[Meaning] Salutations to Brahm Ānanda Ātmā from whom spring forth sprays of bliss in heaven and who is the life of all.

To realize this Self is the ideal of us all. Unless we have come to this Self-realization, we cannot have fullest consciousness of our being and merge with the universal self (Brahman) to attain eternal happiness. Vedic seekers have evolved so far as to have a glimpse of this state in what is called the mystic experience sporadically experienced by some. This experience is different from the three well known states - the waking, dream and sleep - called fourth (turīya). In this state we have some far-fetched likeness of the Divinity that we are.

नैतज्जाग्रन्न च स्वप्नं संकल्पानामसंभवात्।
सुषुप्तभावो नाप्येतदभावाज्जडता स्थितेः।।

योगवासिष्ठ, 6/1.124.25

[Meaning] This is neither the state of waking, nor dreaming being the absence of any thought process, nor it is the state of deep sleep being the absence of ignorance and insensibility.

परिपूर्णार्णवप्रख्या न वा गोचरमेति नः।
नोपमानमुपादत्ते नानुपधावति रंजनम्।। योगवासिष्ठ, 5.64.48
तुर्या चेत्प्राप्यते दृष्टिस्तत्तया सोपमीयते।। योगवासिष्ठ, 5.64.49

[Meaning] This is the state of perfect fullness of soul like vast ocean, which is not attained by us, which is beyond all comparison and all human delights. It can only be compared to turīya state.

Right Information-The only key to Self realization: According to Indian philosophers, Paramātmā is of the nature of Jñāna.

आत्मसंवित्तिरूपम् – 6/1.29.129

[Meaning] God is of the form of knowledge.

So, the right information is the only way to Self realization.

ऋते ज्ञानात् न मुक्तिः।
ṛte jñānāt na muktiḥ.

[Meaning] Self realization is not possible without right information.

Seekers talk about several other methods of Self realization like asceticism, pilgrimage etc. But Yogavāsiṣṭha emphatically denies the fruitfulness of other methods. It says that asceticism, pilgrimage, distribution of alms, yajñas, bathing in sacred rives, reading the Scriptures, performance of prescribed duties are of no avail in Self realization.

न तीर्थेन न दानेन न स्नानेन न विद्यया।
न ध्यानेन न योगेन न तपोभिर्न चाध्वरैः।।

योगवासिष्ठ, 6/2.174.24

[Meaning] The pilgrimage, work of charity, bathing in sacred rivers or on sacred occasions, professional or skill education in a college or university, concentration, yoga, asceticism and yajñas are of no avail in self-realisation.

न शास्त्रान्न गुरोर्वाक्यान्न दानान्नेश्वरार्चनात्।
एष सर्वपदातीतो बोधः संप्राप्यते परः।। योगवासिष्ठ, 6/2.197.18

[Meaning] The knowledge of Śāstras, teachings of a Guru, charities, worship of personal Gods and Goddesses cannot help self realization.

Yogavāsiṣṭha observes that Bhakti or devotion to any personal God or teacher is not required and is not of much avail in Self realization. Only Jñāna (right information or knowledge) leads to Vijñāna (Self realization). Any form of fictitious cult or idol worship rather than attainment of spiritual knowledge, are subject to endless misery.

आत्मसंवित्तिरूपं तु त्यक्त्वा देवार्चनं जनाः।
कृत्रिमार्चासु ये सक्ताश्चिरं क्लेशं भजन्ति ते।।

योगवासिष्ठ, 6/1.29.129

[Meaning] Soul (God) is of the form of knowledge (and is to be worshipped as such) by forsaking the adoration of idols. Those that are devoted to any form of fictitious cult, are subjected to endless misery.

In fact, the idol worshippers have been compared with little children playing with their dolls.

बालक्रीडोपमं च ते अध्यात्मध्यानादृते ब्रह्मकुर्वन्तो देवपूजनम्। 6/1.29.130

On the question of as to what is the best method of the worship of Brahma, the treatise further maintains that Brahma should be worshipped by accumulation of knowledge.

ज्ञानार्जनेनाविरतं पूजनीयः स सर्वदा – 6/1.29.131

True *pūjā* is considered to be the meditation of pure Paramātmā (Brahma) and not otherwise, since the Brahma is the intelligent and everlasting.

त्वमेतच्चेतनाकाशमात्मानं जीवमव्ययम्।
स्वभावं विद्धि न त्वन्यः पूज्यः पूजात्मपूजनम्।। 6/1.29.132

Paramātmā is not to be worshipped with the help of external means like flowers and frankincense.

अबहिः साधनासाध्यम् – 30.31

Yogavāsiṣṭha also discards the concept of worship of mere natural and use of flowers and incense sticks in worship.

नातिदेवार्चने योग्यः पुष्पधूपचयो महान्। 6/1.30.4

Yogavāsiṣṭha, describes the act of idol worship as unlearned, simple as those of children and childish.

अव्युत्पन्नधियो ये हि बालपेलवचेतसः।
कृत्रिमार्चामयं तेषां देवार्चनमुदाहृत्तम्।। 6/1.30.5

In fact, it is due only to lack of understanding that a person worships with flowers, etc. and attribute the Paramātmā to false images of their own making.

शमवोधद्यभावे हि पुष्पाद्यैर्वार्चयन्ति हि।
मिथ्यैव कल्पितैरेतमाकारे कल्पितात्मके।। 6/1.30.6

Yogavāsiṣṭha unleashes scathing attacks on idols as to how the idols may be called as Gods, who having their hands and feet, are yet devoid of their consciousness which is the pith of body.

पादपाण्यादिमानन्यो यो वा देवः प्रकल्प्यते।
संविन्मात्रादृते ब्रह्मन्किसार किल कथ्यताम्।। 6/1.30.19

It is through right information alone that the individual can divinize himself/herself. Right information is the only way to Self realization.

अस्य देवाधिदेवस्य परस्य परमात्मनः।
ज्ञानादेव परा सिद्धिर्न त्वनुष्ठानदुःखतः।।
अत्र ज्ञानमनुष्ठानं न त्वन्यदुपयुज्यते।
मृगतृष्णाजलभ्रान्तिशांतौ चेदं निरुपितम्।। योगवासिष्ठ, 3.6.1–2

[Meaning] The realization of God of Gods is possible only through the right knowledge of Him, and not by the rigour of ritual practices. Here nothing is need than the culture and practice of divine knowledge, and thereby the truth being known, one views the errors of the world, as a satiate traveler looks at a mirage in a clear light.

Yogavāsiṣṭha says emphatically that unless and until an individual is prepared oneself for Self realization, he/she cannot achieve it. Oneself is one's own enemy or friend. If one doesn't want to save himself, there is no remedy.

आत्मैव ह्यात्मनो बन्धुरात्मैव रिपुरात्मनः।
आत्मात्मना न चेत्त्रातस्तदुपायोऽस्ति नेतरः।।

योगवासिष्ठ, 6/2.162.18

[Meaning] Oneself is one's own friend and enemy. If one doesn't want to save himself, there is no remedy.

What is not attained from within can never be attained from without from all the three worlds.

अभ्यासवैराग्ययुतादाक्रान्तेन्द्रियपन्नगात्।
नात्मनः प्राप्यते यत्तत्प्राप्यते न जगत्त्रयात्।।

योगवासिष्ठ, 5.43.18

[Meaning] What is not attained by oneself through one's own constant efforts accompanied by self resignation and self control, cannot be attained through anything else in all the three worlds.

The real God to be worshipped resides in one's own self. Any other God needs not be worshipped at all. Those who leaving the God residing in their own heart, go to other God, are like those who, having thrown away the precious gems they had in their own pocket, desire to collect ordinary stone.

संत्यज्य हृद्गुहेशानं देवमन्यं प्रयान्ति ये।
ते रत्नमभिवांछन्ति त्यक्तहस्तस्थकौस्तुभाः।। योगवासिष्ठ, 5.8.14

[Meaning] Those leaving the God residing in their own heart, go to other God, are like those who, having thrown away the precious gems in their hands, desire to collect ordinary stone.

Gods, even when pleased with long devotion, cannot bestow knowledge on those who are devoid of thought process. As such gross idolaters can have no salvation, which is to be had by knowledge only. Blind faith is of no good without thoughtfulness.

चिरमाराधितोऽप्येष परमप्रीतिमानपि।
नाविचारवतो ज्ञानं दातुं शक्नोति माधवः।। योगवासिष्ठ, 5.43.10

[Meaning] And though this God may be pleased with prolonged service and devout worship, yet he is unable to confer knowledge to one devoid of thought process.

Devotion to God like Viṣṇu is invented for those who are intellectually challenged like children.

शास्त्रयत्नविचारेभ्यो मूर्खाणां प्रपलायिनाम् ।
कल्पिता वैष्णवी भक्तिः प्रवृत्त्यर्थं शुभस्थितौ।।

योगवासिष्ठ, 5.43.20

[Meaning] The devotion to God like Viṣṇu is invented for those who are intellectually challenged and absconding from the discussion of Śāstras, so that they may have a tendency to be on the right path.

The artificial ways of worshipping God are only for those whose minds are not fully grown up.

अव्युत्पन्नधियो ये हि बालपेलवचेतसः।
कृत्रिमार्चामयं तेषां देवार्चनमुदाहृतम् ।।

योगवासिष्ठ, 6/1.30.5

[Meaning] Artificial ways of worshipping God are only for those whose minds are not grown up like children.

It is only because of right information alone that the God residing within heart can be realized.

अस्य देवाधिदेवस्य परस्य परमात्मनः।
ज्ञानादेव परा सिद्धिर्न त्वनुष्ठानदुःखतः।।योगवासिष्ठ, 3.6.1

[Meaning] This supreme God and can be realized only through right information and not through rigour of religious rituals and practices.

Even a teacher, however wise he may be, cannot divinize an individual who is not thoughtful and make efforts accordingly. If a spiritual teacher can raise one up without one's own effort, why does not he raise up a bull, an elephant or a camel?

गुरुश्चेदुद्धरत्यज्ञमात्मीयात्पौरुषादृते।
उष्ट्रं दान्तं बलीवर्दं तत्कस्मान्नोद्धरत्यसौ।।

योगवासिष्ठ, 5.43.16

[Meaning] If a spiritual teacher raise up a fool without his (fool's) own effort, why does not he raise up a bull, an elephant or a camel.

Whatever wherever is achieved by anyone that is through his own efforts and power.

यद्यदासाद्यते किंचित्केनचित्क्वचिदेव हि।
स्वशक्तिसंप्रवृत्त्या तल्लभ्यते नान्यतः क्वचित् ।।

योगवासिष्ठ, 5.43.13

[Meaning] Whatever wherever is achieved by whosoever that is through his own efforts and power and not through some other means.

Yogavasiṣṭha is very much clear that nothing can be achieved either through teacher or God.

न हरेर्न गुरोर्नार्थात्किंचिदासाद्यते महत् ।
आक्रान्तमनसः स्वस्माद्यदासादितमात्मनः ।।योगवासिष्ठ, 3.43.17

[Meaning] Nothing can be achieved either through God or teacher. It is through the power of one's own mind that anything good for one's self is achieved.

There is lot of debate on the issue whether an action is to be renunciated or not for Self realization. Shankaracharya, in this regard, lays emphasis on the renunciation of active household-life for Self realization. According to him, tyāga and saṁnyāsa seems to be quite indispensable for Self realization. Early Buddhism is also a religion of Bhikṣukas (recluses). Bhagvad Gita, however, seems to preach that the duties enjoined upon us by the Śāstras are not to be given up. They are to be performed without attachment or personal motive. Absolute renunciation is neither possible nor required by Krishna. Similar view is expressed by Swami Dayanand. According to him, a person cannot live without doing actions. The main emphasis is upon selfish motive behind action. Both Gita and Swami Dayanand lay stress upon actions should be done selflessly with the intention of altruistic welfare. When actions are done with the notion of altruistic welfare, one remains detached and such actions do not become obstacles in self realization. On the other hand action performed with selfish motive become obstacles in self realization. The View of Gita and Swami Dayananda is also supported by Yogavāsiṣṭha. Accordingly, performing or giving up any kind of action, whether it be religious, moral or worldly, is immaterial for Self realization. (6.199.31)

न क्रियायाः परित्यागो न क्रियाया समाश्रयः ।
नाचारेषु समारम्भविचित्रफलपालयः ।। योगवासिष्ठ, 6/2.199.31

[Meaning] Neither giving up or performing an action, nor customary duties material in self realization.

It is foolish to believe that action can be renounced. Life itself is an action. Human being's other name is action. As long as one is living, one is acting.

कर्मैव पुरुषो राम पुरुषस्यैव कर्मता।
एते ह्यभिन्ने विद्धि त्वं यथा तुहिनशीतते।। योगवासिष्ठ, 6/2.28.8

[Meaning] O Ram! action is man and man is action. Both are inseparable like ice and coldness.

अस्य राघव सूक्ष्मस्य कर्मणो वेदनात्मनः।
कस्त्यागः किमनुष्ठानं यावद्देहमिति स्थितम्।।

योगवासिष्ठ, 6/2.2.31

[Meaning] Ram! It is no way possible to avoid our actions as long as the body exists.

त्यागो हि कर्मणां तस्मादादेहं नोपपद्यते।

योगवासिष्ठ, 6/2.2.42

[Meaning] No one is exempted from action as long as he/she lives with sensible body.

यावदायुरियं राम निश्चितं स्पन्दते तनुः।
तद्यथा प्राप्तमव्यग्रं स्पन्दतामपरेण किम् ।।

योगवासिष्ठ, 6/2.199.5

[Meaning] So long as there is life, body is in action, O Ram! As such, necessary actions must be performed without hesitation, instead of unwanted ones.

Renunciation of physical and worldly activities is impossible. The root of action is desire or will. That is really to be controlled in order to save oneself from the binding effect of action.

मूलं स्वकर्मणः संविन्मनसो वासनात्मकः।

योगवासिष्ठ, 6/2.2.43

[Meaning] The root of action is desire or will.

Personal desires or will are to be given up and not actions. They, who give up external actions without having given up desires for them, effect a renunciation which is no renunciation at all. The devil of renunciation devours those fools who attempt that renunciation of actions which is no renunciation at all.

अत्यागं त्यागमिति ये कुर्वते व्यर्थबोधिनः।

सा भुंक्ते तान्पशूनज्ञानकर्मत्यागपिशाचिका।।

योगवासिष्ठ, 6/2.3.26

[Meaning] They who give up external actions without having given up desires for them, effect a renunciation which is no renunciation at all. The devil of renunciation devours those who attempt that renunciation of actions which is no renunciation at all.

For Self realization, according to Yogavāsiṣtha, one has not even to go to a forest, renouncing the worldly life and activities. The busy home life is no bar to Self realization. Renouncing the activities of life and residing in a forest away from worldly disturbances do not in the least help one whose mind is fickle and restless. The home is itself is a quiet forest for whose mind is peaceful, whereas a forest is like a crowded city for one who is not at peace within.

गेहमेवोपशान्तस्य विजनं दूरकाननम् ।
अशान्तस्याप्यरण्यानि विजना सजना पुरी।। योगवासिष्ठ, 6/2.3.38

[Meaning] The home is a quiet forest for whose mind is peaceful, whereas a forest is like a crowded city for one whose mind is not peaceful.

The story of the queen Cuḍāla and her husband Śikhidhvaja in the Nirvāṇa Prakaraṇa is a beautiful illustration of this act. Vasiṣṭ ha is very emphatic on this point. According to him, a wise man should prefer not to retire from the busy life of the world, although it is in no way binding upon him.

राजन्यावदयं देहस्तावन्मुक्तधियामपि।
यथाप्राप्तक्रियात्यागो रोचते न स्वभावतः।।

योगवासिष्ठ, 5.26.16

[Meaning] O King! As long as this body is there, one should prefer not to retire from busy life of the world even through his/her mind is freed from everything.

Most of the liberated living men (Jīanmuktas) rule over their kingdoms, and give the benefit of their wisdom to others. Thus, according to Yogavāsiṣtha, Neither devotion to any personal God nor renunciation of actions is therefore a means to divinization.

---

[i] The scholars who try to work out the date of Rāma around 5000-6000 BC on the basis of planetarium soft ware forget that this combination of starts and planets is the latest one and the same combination is repeated every 25920 years.

[ii] Dr. Ravi Prakash Arya (1998). Vālmiki Rāmāyaṇa edited with English Translation, (Four Vols.), Delhi

www.ingramcontent.com/pod-product-compliance
Lightning Source LLC
Chambersburg PA
CBHW031439040426
42444CB00006B/886
* 9 7 8 8 1 8 7 7 1 0 9 1 2 *